my father's kites

ALLISON
JOSEPH

PRAISE FOR MY FATHER'S KITES

I want poems to take me where I haven't been before. I want them to invite me to leap into some other world. The poems in Allison Joseph's My Father's Kites do just that. The poems here are achingly, tenderly, artfully realized, and they create a world that is both typical and completely unto itself. Here a young woman considers her deceased father's troubled life and her own uneasy relationship with him, and, in almost the exact center of "What the Eye Beholds," the thirty-four poem sonnet sequence at the heart of My Father's Kites, she recognizes that "Words cannot undo what's done." There is regret but also freedom in the recognition that some things cannot be fixed. And somehow Joseph's words also do what had been left undone. These poems say what had been kept unsaid, gather all the resentment and longing, all the irritation and adoration, into a richly nuanced world.

~ JEFF MOCK

"Tell me about the poet," urges Allison Joseph in the very first line of her remarkable new collection—and it is with insight, honesty and extraordinary technical skill that she accomplishes exactly this. My Father's Kites is a self-revelatory collection of carefully wrought, jewel-like poems that explore the often paradoxical complexities of family relationships. Her strategy is tightly linked to her remarkable expertise as a formalist—a gift that becomes most evident in "What the Eye Beholds," a series of sonnets about her father's flamboyant life, his gradual "dereliction," his inevitable early death, and its poignant aftermath. The arc of this sequence, flanked as it is by graceful villanelles and rondeaus, is as fluid and symmetrical as the poems themselves. I cannot think of another contemporary poet who has done a finer job of combining form and content, to dazzling effect.

~ MARILYN TAYLOR

Allison Joseph's father used to construct amazing kites when she was a child—"makeshift diamonds, homemade contraptions"—that somehow managed to transcend her Bronx neighborhood and sail into the sky. Now, in her brilliant memoir of her father's life, My Father's Kites, she, too, constructs her own kites, soaring sonnets and pantoums and villanelles that capture elusive memories of the troubled but imaginative man who shaped her youth. Superbly executed, part family history and part homage, Allison Joseph's My Father's Kites strings the frail human voice across the forceful lines of her verse to summon her absent father back from the dead.

~ MAURA STANTON

PRAISE FOR WORLDLY PLEASURES

Worldly Pleasures is a book about pushing past tribulations to seek joy; in play, in friendship, in relationship. Ranging from a memorable series of character portraits to sensual love poems, Allison Joseph's fifth full-length collection finds, in its clear, smooth lines, a way to celebrate the world despite its difficulties. *Worldly Pleasures* further establishes Joseph as one of the leading poets of her young generation.

~ KEVIN WALZER

PRAISE FOR VOICE

Sassy and funky, serious and sly, the poems in Allison Joseph's *Voice* travel through a rich and varied landscape. From childhood griefs to adult desires, the classroom to the bar, these poems cut and cajole, tackling the most serious and the most sultry with a graceful eloquence. Like a soloist who rises above the rest of the choir, the voice in these poems peals with clarity and beauty, leading us from a place of familiarity smack dab into the sublime.

~ STACEY LYNN BROWN

Praise for *In Every Seam*

The poet's double vision, recalling the events of her life and framing them in history, is a large part of the strength of this book . . . Throughout this book, Joseph presents the events of daily life both plainly and transcendently, as if to summon up the entire cultural setting in which they take place. Her tone and vision maintain a strong balance through which she sees both the "sorry garbage" and the strength and will towards survival of those who inhabit it.

~Judith Johnson, *Women's Review of Books*

These poems point to the strong materials needed to make ourselves whole in the modern world. They alert us to the seams we must tug at to see into ourselves.

~Yusef Komunyakaa

my father's kites

ALLISON
JOSEPH

STEEL TOE BOOKS

BOWLING GREEN, KENTUCKY

ISBN 978-0-9824169-2-1

STEEL TOE BOOKS
Western Kentucky University
Department of English
1906 College Heights Blvd. #11086
Bowling Green, KY 42101-1086
steeltoebooks.com

COVER ART
"Kite at Fort Stevens" by Andrew Wallace, 2007

AUTHOR PHOTOGRAPH
Self-portrait by the author

COVER AND BOOK DESIGN
Molly McCaffrey

In memory of Everest Michael Joseph, my father;
in celebration of Jon Charles Tribble, my husband

Contents

one

two

what the eye beholds

three

one

Bio Note

Tell me about the poet.
Does she embrace her culture,
celebrate her sexuality,
reaffirm her heritage,
practice semiotics,
declare her independence
from heretofore influential
yet now inconsequential masters?
Does she anger all the right
angels, misbehave in the nicest
way, make wondrous
the quotidian, elevating the ordinary
so far into the transcendent
that we are left shaking
her celestial dust
off our boot soles?
Does she live on three acres
with two kids that inspire
all she does, a nurturing husband
who sells spy novels to support
her late night bouts with
immortality? Does she live
urban and alone with two cats
or two dogs or two rabbits
or one rabbit with two ferrets,
or two ferrets and no cats?
Is she an MFA, a PhD, an M.S.W.,
an MAT with a specialization
in ESL? Was she born in '67,

or '47, or '43 or '63;
is her hair red or blonde
or permed or dyed or natural?
Does she wear feathered earrings,
combat boots, slinky boas,
faux fur? Is she a potter,
a dancer, a flutist, a pianist,
a gourmet chef, a chess grand master?
Is she eligible for Mensa?
Is she nobody's mother,
nobody's wife?
Tell me about the poet.

ON NOT WANTING TO WRITE A MEMOIR

What's there to write? I had the kind of youth
I'll need the rest of life to figure out.
Forgive me if I won't tell you the truth.

My memory is insecure. I have no proof
that what I claim is true. There's always doubt.
What's there to write? I had the kind of youth

where memory's a shifting realm. We moved
before I knew what moving was about.
Forgive me if I won't tell you the truth.

Three countries, three households, three roofs.
Three homes where I could play, or fall, or pout.
What's there to write? I had the kind of youth

that surfaces in dreams, not tamed, uncouth—
each fear or happiness of equal clout.
Forgive me if I won't tell you the truth.

Some memories lurk deep, in bone and tooth,
with consequences I can do without.
What's there to write? I had *that* kind of youth.
Forgive me if I don't tell you the truth.

Elegy for the Personal Letter

I miss the rumpled corners of correspondence,
the ink blots and crossouts that show
someone lives on the other end, a person
whose hands make errors, leave traces.
I miss fine stationary, its raised elegant
lettering prominent on creamy shades of ivory
or pearl grey. I even miss hasty notes
dashed off on notebook paper, edges
ragged as their scribbled messages—
can't much write now—thinking of you.
When letters come now, they are formatted
by some distant computer, addressed
to *Occupant* or *To the family living at—*
meager greetings at best,
salutations made by committee.
Among the glossy catalogs
and one time only offers
the bills and invoices,
letters arrive so rarely now that I drop
all other mail to the floor when
an envelope arrives and the handwriting
is actual handwriting, the return address
somewhere I can locate on any map.
So seldom is it that letters come
that I stop everything else
to identify the scrawl that has come this far—
the twist and the whirl of the letters,
the loops of the numerals. I open

those envelopes first, forgetting
the claim of any other mail,
hoping for news I could not read
in any other way but this.

GREETING CARDS

What compelled me to buy them,
mail them to a father who would not
mail one back, despite the short span

between my birthday, his? Why did I
read those rhymed verses so carefully,
trying to find the blandest good wishes

among the pale envelopes,
the flimsy cards with their scenes
of fishing boats and mallard ducks

designed to make the eyes
of even the most callous father
mist over in reverie? At the end,

my father's eyes were dim from diabetes,
the heavy stone of a magnifying glass
by his bedside in the house

he'd made his daughters too frightened
to come home to. I sent those cards
more for myself than for him,

hoping to provoke something better
than anger, or silence. After his death,
we found the cards secreted away,

and I bound them with a rubber band,

wanted to offer them as proof of love
to every funeral home doubter,

fanning them out in my hands.
I read my own handwriting
beneath the series of postmarks

as if it were not mine, but the scrawl
of a stranger writing the name
of someone she never met.

When I turned them over,
I saw why he'd kept them—
he'd written rows and rows

of lottery numbers in a hand
so beautiful and deliberate
I could almost forget

their mathematics of addiction,
promise of payoff so tempting
my father kept straining his vision

to pick the winning numbers,
long after the damage
any windfall could repair.

MY FATHER'S KITES

were crude assemblages of paper sacks and twine,
amalgams of pilfered string and whittled sticks,
twigs pulled straight from his garden, dry patch

of stony land before our house only he
could tend into beauty, thorny roses goaded
into color. How did he make those makeshift

diamonds rise, grab ahold of the wind to sail
into sky like nothing in our neighborhood
of dented cars and stolid brick houses could?

It wasn't through faith or belief in otherworldly
grace, but rather a metaphor from moving
on a street where cars rusted up on blocks,

monstrously immobile, and planes, bound
for that world we could not see, roared
above our heads, our houses pawns

in a bigger flight path. How tricky the launch
into air, the wait for the right eddy to lift
our homemade contraptions into the sullen

blue sky above us, our eyes stinging
with the glut of the sun. And the sad tangle
after flight, collapse of grocery bags

and broken branches, snaggle of string

I still cannot unfurl. Father, you left me
with this unsated need to find the most

delicately useful of breezes, to send
myself into the untenable, balance my weight
as if on paper wings, a flutter then fall,

a stutter back to earth, an elastic sense
of being and becoming forged in our front
yard, your hand over mine over balled string.

two
what the eye beholds

LONG DISTANCE NEWS

The instant I picked up and said hello
I heard a loud, sharp knock at my front door.
A city cop I'd never seen before
passed me a note, then quickly turned to go.
Scrawled on the note: call Henry Fabio—
my father's friend? What should I call him for?
I said out loud. I wanted to ignore
this ominous coincidence, although
I knew I had to pick back up the phone
and listen to my cousin's sober voice:
It's Daddy Joe. He's gone. She'd said the words
I feared she'd say, her voice resigned in tone
as she told me the news. I had no choice.
I couldn't push away what I'd just heard.

In the Classroom

I vowed I wouldn't cry in front of class;
I'd be professional, tell them what I
could barely tell myself. I could have lied,
or let my source of trouble go unasked
by students who knew little of a past
I'd only talk about to make a point,
to illustrate some alternate viewpoint.
But there, in front of them, the tears came fast,
as fast as I could say, *my father's died.*
And as I tried to get each sentence out,
my students rose to hug me, or confide
that they'd had losses too, known grief and doubt.
I'd hoped not to appear undignified,
but death was what I couldn't speak about.

FIRST CONSULTATION:
ORTIZ FUNERAL HOME

How does one plan some sort of funeral
for someone who thought God the biggest hoax?
The funeral director tries to coax
us into buying more, but cynical,
we tell him we don't think it's natural
to purchase prayer cards for a man who'd joke
as his own dying wife sang to evoke
the power of the Lord through spirituals.
He'd laugh, declare no God was waiting for
his kind and faithful servants here on earth
to join him in his paradise above.
The God our mother praised our dad deplored.
We choose a simple casket, for its dearth
of symbols of a god's redemptive love.

Personal Effects: Bronx County Courthouse, December 1997

His credit cards were in a plastic case,
along with jewelry, pairs of gold cufflinks.
A state health badge revealed my father's face—
an older man, but still too young to sink
down to the floor to die at sixty-five.
Efficient cops, they made me sign each page
of a typed report of what he'd had alive:
the house's deed, license with proof of age
he'd turned just weeks before. No time to mourn
with pages slipping past for me to sign,
the paperwork that seemed already worn,
a claim to the remains he'd left behind.
And then I passed the cops the page they sought:
the funeral receipt, the coffin bought.

THE FIRST MOMENT

The moment I first glimpsed my father dead
I thought the tears would flow immediately,
his head against the coffin's silk. Instead
I felt a laugh leap from my mouth, from me—
a burst of mirth, relief, and bitterness.
He looked too good for death, too calm, serene,
reclining there as if a little rest
was all he'd showed up for. I didn't mean
to laugh out loud, but strangely I was proud
to be the child of such a handsome man
who'd stir out of this sleep if something loud
went off, some noisy crash nobody planned.
A kid ran up to touch this man who seemed
to be wrapped up inside some lasting dream.

IN THE FUNERAL PARLOUR

The silent woman at my father's wake
avoids my gaze, as if she is not here.
There isn't anything that she should fear—
I won't approach to share in her heartache,
or tell her that my father's great mistake
was living with a heart grown so severe
his daughters lost all hope they might endear
themselves to him. So thin, she might just break
under the weight of what we won't discuss.
No word seems right for her—she's not his friend,
so sad and plain, she's no petite mistress.
She's just another woman he could bend,
manipulate with widower's distress.
For both our sakes, I'm glad this is the end.

COUNTRYMEN

My father's college classmates shake my hand;
they smell of alcohol, have rheumy eyes.
They stare at me, exclaim, then recognize
the features that remind them of the man
who'd left behind their small obscure island,
just as they'd done. They each seem slight in size,
their hands atremble as they eulogize
their comrade from that faraway homeland
I've seen in person only once. They say
he loved his girls, that he was proud
of all his daughters had become. I don't
reply, just nod my head. I'm here to play
the role of grieving child who's not allowed
to speak of memory's truth when others won't.

Before the Burial

No pastor came to greet us with a speech,
no sermon made death easy to accept.
No organist, not there, it wasn't church,
but someplace more morose, a place adept
at dispatching the dead. No gospel choir
sang harmony for us in brillant gowns,
no collared priest wore somber dull attire,
no widow, clad in black, held her head down.
Instead, I read aloud some clumsy words,
some abstract sentiments I wrote in rhyme,
a small gesture to make me more secure
in grief, since Father left no plans behind.
So little reassurance in my verse,
no power to avoid that ride, that hearse.

How Sweet the Sound

At graveside someone starts to sing aloud:
*Amazing grace, how sweet the sound...*I think
about the song, its words profound
but far from music Father would have picked
for this event. He would have had us sing
a song that didn't mention saving grace,
denying any kind of lord or king.
He'd tell us all, a smirk upon his face,
to play some jumping jazz or raucous blues:
an Armstrong strut or John Lee Hooker dirge,
the kind of songs a man like him would choose,
no Christian hymns for him, no sudden urge
to have salvation make this day less grim.
Imagine how he'd laugh to mock this hymn.

POSTMORTEM

White business cards, imprinted with your name,
expensive stationary, custom-made.
Twin stacks of bills, demanding to be paid,
collection agencies' persistent claims.
Each letter's language sounds almost the same—
some pleas, some threats, some terse and brusque
    tirades,
monotonous as records we once played
on our console stereo. My mother's picture, framed,
recalls another world of black and white,
where you sold everything you thought you could—
a salesman's smile, but shaky guarantees.
But now, no books of get rich quick advice
can do my father good. You never would
stop scheming profits, planning strategies.

Dress Code

No one could tell my father what to do:
how he should dress, where he should spend his cash.
He loved designer suits—the deft panache
of jackets, vests, and trousers purchased new,
and famous fragrances—the bottles grew
from few until the crowd of flasks would clash
and tumble from his dresser, down to crash
and leak out on the carpet, knocked askew.
The silky ties, the pointy leather shoes
he'd polish to a bright demanding shine
with strokes both swift and sure, precisely done.
Gold cufflinks, tie tacks, slim silver pens to sign
the flourish of his signature. He'd shun
the plain, clothes other men saw fit to choose.

WHAT THE EYE BEHOLDS

I find your camera, a knockoff brand
called Nikanon you bought hot off the street.
There's film in it, a roll made bittersweet
by knowing that your death, swift and unplanned,
assures me I will never understand
your life. It's so elusive, incomplete,
and I can't help but feel I'm obsolete—
our bond has disappeared, like sleight of hand.
The camera's photos show another life:
a birthday party for a new girlfriend,
her children gathered close to celebrate.
Was this the one you loved just like a wife?
I put the pictures down, and can't pretend
to know my father's world: his loves, his hates.

HOME OFFICE

My father stays at home because he can;
he watches Elmer chasing Bugs on screen.
He's not about to work for any man
except himself—he'll make his own routines,
determine when he'll shower, shave, get clean,
put on a suit and tie that will impress.
To clients, it's important to be seen
as stylish both in character and dress—
those self-employed in sales need more finesse
than those content to work from nine to five,
their every speech assured and effortless
to make each client see a man who thrives
on meeting every customer's demand,
once he leaves bed to sell what he's got planned.

TEMPERAMENT

My father's voice could go from kind to gruff—
in just a blink, he'd turn from sweet to curt,
his shifts in mood disturbingly abrupt.
I always feared I couldn't do enough
to keep his voice from rising, growing rough
in angry shouts that left me crying, hurt
by curses that pushed out of him in spurts.
I knew that one mistake could make him huff
his threats at me, then stop. I always feared
I'd break a vase or plate; I'd drop a bowl
or trip and crack a treasured serving dish.
He'd yell *you clumsy stupid kid.* I'd clear
the shards of glass. But soon I'd be his girl
again, his favored child, his only wish.

DIABETES

That word, to me, was such a mystery—
an odd disease of needles, insulin,
injections that would pierce my father's skin.
At first I didn't understand when he
would stagger up the stairs, unkempt, dizzy,
as if some fear were quivering within.
His thirst had forced his body to give in.
He'd stumble to the fridge, weak in the knees,
to get some drink to swallow down or else
he'd faint, some juice or soda, something sweet
to calm his sweaty chills and bring him back
to normalcy, to come back to himself.
When he would take his shot and then not eat,
his body paid him back with these attacks.

DEFERRED

> No, it was always money, Mama.
> We just didn't know about it.
>   —*A Raisin in the Sun*

My father loved the role of Walter Lee,
the character that Poitier portrayed—
a black man fighting for his dignity
against a world that wanted him to stay
obsequious and meek. When Walter said,
it was always money, my dad agreed,
quoting the line aloud, nodding his head.
But Walter, like my father, felt the need
to squander money on a faulty scheme.
When Walter lost it all, my father turned
away from the TV. He never seemed
to want to know what lesson Walter learned.
No need to keep the television on
with Walter now reduced to Mama's son.

FLASHBACK: CALVARY HOSPITAL, 1985

My sister says our mother's final hours
had her in pain my father couldn't stand,
though she would call his name, a last demand
she moaned despite her dimming power.
She kept repeating "Joe" from sheer willpower,
my father's nickname like a reprimand
when Mother murmured it. Her voice began
a chant it couldn't stop. He was too dour
to comfort her like no pain killer would,
to touch her withered hand and smile
the kind of smile we wear when hope is gone.
If I had gotten home in time I could
have listened to those cries, though it's futile
to say now. Words cannot undo what's done.

LUXURY CAR

The car he loved the most? Mercedes Benz.
He craved its ambiance, the way it would
demand attention as he took the road,
a sleek authority that did not end
if he had unpaid bills he didn't send,
if sales orders weren't coming like they should.
My father couldn't deny that regal hood,
those stylish hubcaps, symbols of a blend
of pricey taste and German workmanship.
But his machines were rusting metal hulks
he'd buy at auctions, bargains secondhand,
autos far too old for speeding trips,
too fragile to move quickly with such bulk,
unable to survive such rough demands.

GRADUATION DAY, KENYON COLLEGE, 1988

How they give a little black girl like you
a Jim Crow Ransom prize? my father asked
that graduation day. The senior class
milled happily, not sure yet what to do,
degrees in hand. My father never knew
who John Crowe Ransom was. Still he unmasked
the whiteness of that place, its storied past
replete with narrow-minded people who
he thought he'd wisely taught me to despise.
Now I had claimed a place among them all,
the very whites he'd tried to demonize
for years. My newly earned degree felt small
and insignificant. He thought my prize
did nothing more than signal my shortfall.

MY FATHER'S HAND MIRROR

I hold the mirror as my father did,
see imperfections, blemishes and lines.
A handsome man, he'd tried in vain to rid
himself of graying hairs that intertwined
themselves among the stronger, darker strands.
He'd make me tweeze away the silver hairs—
I'd use a comb, then section with my hands
to pluck away what I found nestled there,
the evidence of age he couldn't face.
A child, I didn't fully comprehend
his constant nightly efforts to erase
what time had done, what he could not amend.
But now I glimpse the lines under my eyes,
can feel that doubt he knew begin its rise.

DERELICTION

I wasn't there to help you when you fell,
your body slumping down with such a thud,
our downstairs tenant came up in alarm,
asked if you needed help. Not there to tell
you what to do, to try and stanch the blood
that stained the carpet black. Your weakened arms
could not support your weight. Your body's harm
would go unchecked, a painful flood
you didn't want to face. You wouldn't let
him take you to the hospital. You shunned
his aid, refused when he tried to compel
you to care about your life, take this threat
to heart. I'll never know your last regrets,
too far from home to make my father well.

DAUGHTERS CLEANING HOUSE

We give away your clothes to charity,
throw out receipts you'd kept since '71.
Why you held on so tight's a mystery,
as if in letting go you'd be undone,
and everything you'd bought unauthorized.
We find new photos of your other life,
snapshots of girlfriends we don't recognize.
Not one of them, we learn, was going to be your wife—
you'd told each one that they could never mean
as much as Mother meant to you for years.
Still, it unnerves us to observe these scenes
of other women bending close to hear
the tales you'd spin, forsaken widower,
revealing truth in versions you preferred.

FORMER BEDROOM

I cough and sweep away the dust of years—
beneath my broom the dirt accumulates,
the carpet rich with grime and stains from spills
my father never cleaned. Remembered fears
rush back to me as I survey this room:
my mother's gospel hymns, mournful, sedate
those years the thriving cancer made her ill,
my father's spurts of angry words. He'd fume
while she would pray, her halting breath
a whispering that made him so irate
he had no heart for what her God could will.
He'd tell her *there's no life after your death.*
I cough and sweep this dust that stings my eyes,
each motion setting free their musty lives.

ATOP THE CONSOLE

My father placed my mother's photograph
alone atop our console stereo,
her vibrant face surrounded by thick curls,
mouth open in a smile, as if to laugh
at some small secret only she could know,
before life in the States, before her girls
grew into womanhood, before the whirl
of years, before she had to undergo
the bouts with chemotherapy, the pills.
After her death, he kept this curio
so every other woman could feel half
as vital as my mother was until
the cancer crept inside her, made her ill.
That photo's sorrow worked on Dad's behalf.

DOMICILE

You left behind a house you couldn't tend,
three floors of rooms that you could not maintain,
a backyard overgrown with brush and weeds,
a buckle in the roof gone unrestrained.
Was this the house I spent my childhood in—
where Father, you grew roses in the front?
That soil's now gritty earth, arid, so thin
just ghost bushes survive, ragged and blunt.
Inside, the staircase rails are falling out,
some wholly gone. Outside, the brick columns
that fenced the front yard in lie strewn about
from when you backed your car right into them,
missing the driveway's mark. You never moved
the bricks, defying those who disapproved.

PARADE OF CARTOON STARS

I watch a cartoon cat pursue a mouse,
remember how you'd grin at their hijinks.
Your cackle would resound throughout the house,
such pleasure in their animated tricks
of booby traps or guns or powder kegs.
You'd sing the Jetsons' theme, or the Flinstones',
or laugh at Olive Oyl, her scrawny legs.
I didn't think it weird to find you home,
amused by Jerry Mouse and Tom the Cat,
Quick Draw Mc Graw and Huckleberry Hound,
not wondering where other dads were at
but knowing mine preferred to stay homebound.
Those cartoon characters were all that moved,
at least until the sales climate improved.

PROFESSIONS

When friends would ask *what does your father do?*
I'd hesitate, not sure what I could say.
Now that he's gone, I find his resume—
a typed-up list of all that he'd pursued,
distinctive men he'd struggled to become:
the advertising man whose slick cachet
could move those goods that others shrugged away,
the real estate exec who'd sell you some
snug plot in Florida, insurance man
who'd guarantee the safety of your life.
But later in the list, a change in plans—
a shift to the profession of his wife,
to work in hospitals where lives expired.
He needed cash, became a nurse for hire.

PRIVATE DUTY NURSE

My sister tells the story of the time
our father came from work an angry man.
He yelled for her as if she'd done some crime,
then roared his one unsettling demand:
Did my check come? She answered no, then watched
his life decline—he'd stay out late to drink
then stumble home to start a shouting match
with her. What brought him to that edge, that brink
he couldn't come back from? Much later on,
we found his daily logs about a case,
his patient notes about somebody's son,
a boy with sickle cell, kidney disease.
For months he'd been the nurse at this boy's side.
Just what had Father lost when that child died?

FATHER'S LINEAGE

My grandmother looked pale, her father white,
and in Grenada that was all it took
to make a woman famous for her looks,
to make her coveted. Her skin as light
as cream, she was the envy and delight
for miles around, a woman never overlooked
when beauty was discussed, a storybook
queen without a king. She married the right
man, handsome catch whose slender poker face
I've seen in only one yellowed snapshot.
My grandmother remained behind as he
departed to make money in the States.
She later learned my grandfather begot
a secret shame: another family.

FIRST PHONE CALL WITH MY UNCLE

His voice sounds like my dad's, but less intense,
familar island accent without strain.
I listen as he patiently explains:
my dad and he were brothers in the sense
they shared a common father, not a home.
My grandfather neglected both his sons—
responsiblities he chose to shun,
a world beyond that island he could roam.
When last I saw my uncle, I was two,
my sister eight. We couldn't say we'd met
this rival Father wanted to forget.
You can't keep bitterness inside of you,
my uncle says, *you can't hold onto it—*
a notion Father never would admit.

A CONVERSATION

My sister hears our father's voice at night,
gruff shouts of "stupid" sounding in her brain,
a fierce unyielding message of disdain
she can't erase. The voice she hears is tight
and unresolved, its terse anger a blight
she can't escape. It's one childhood refrain
she thought would fade away, grow dim and wane
as memories tend to do. Why now this fright,
this echo of contempt caught in her life
now that he's dead and cannot growl her name?
He'd call me clumsy too, I say to her,
small consolation offered for her strife.
How memory holds on to guilt and shame,
the sting of words still making us unsure.

ABSENCE

I miss the man who used to build me kites,
who'd whittle twigs to form a homemade frame,
cut parts from paper bags, add twine or string
to make them flutter far above the height
of apple trees he'd planted in the yard.
I miss the man who made schoolwork a game,
who'd pay me for each spelling test I'd bring
to him, two quarters if the words were hard.
I want that father back who laughed aloud
when I declared I'd run away from home,
who tempted me with Snickers bars, who'd sing
a made-up tune to show the world how proud
he was of me. I want to have that life
we knew before my mother's death, his wife's.

FIRST BIRTHDAY AFTER YOUR DEATH: NOVEMBER 1998

This month I will not pace a card shop's aisles
in search of words that I could send to you:
a birthday card to ship across the miles
in hopes some correspondence might ensue—
a letter in return where you could share
the ordinary details of your life,
not revelations showing how you cared
or mourning for the absence of your wife.
This month I will not wonder if you read
the tepid verses on your birthday card,
the envelope not falling by your bed,
along with other mail you'd disregard.
No longer will I do what I have done;
all hope to read my father's answers gone.

CODA

My father isn't sleeping anymore,
nor is he watching TV shows he's seen
so many times he quotes their dialogue,
nor is he forcing me to do my chores:
weed our rocky garden, go to the store
to fetch his *Daily News*. He hasn't been
in the garage among the waterlogged
suitcases, steamer trunks our family bore
from house to house until we settled here,
a house whose roof he cannot come repair—
his tools abandoned, rusty from disuse.
My father isn't coming up the stairs
to yell my name or tease that I'm adored.
Some other man now wears the clothes he wore.

three

POEM FOR MY GRANDFATHER

You are nothing more to me
than this black and white photo, a history
so recondite my father rarely spoke your name.
Impervious to blame,
you chose instead to flee.

My father never knew this man that he
called father—only a paper decree
told him of his lineage. Was this your aim?
You are nothing more.

These faces, so alike. How much the features agree.
You never knew the hatred, a legacy
of bitterness my father couldn't tame,
blistering until it would maim
my father's life, a life you didn't care to see.
You are nothing more.

ABSENCE WITHOUT LEAVE

So where was I the day my father died?
I'd stayed away for years, in fear of him.
I wasn't next to him, not by his side.

I'd wanted to be free, so never tried
to let him know my choice was not a whim.
So where was I the day my father died?

I lived a life I knew I had to hide,
my father's edicts resolutely grim.
I wasn't next to him, not by his side

when he sunk to the floor. He might have cried
or might have watched his vision going dim.
So where was I the day my father died?

I'd gone too long without him to confide
that I had "married white," to one of "them."
I wasn't next to him, not by his side

to urge him to the doctor, damn his pride.
I do not know how death felt in in his limbs.
So where was I the day my father died?
Not next to him, no daughter by his side.

This Letter Is an Attempt to Collect a Debt

We've yet to hear from you with payment due,
we've waited patiently to get your check.
Your credit privileges won't be renewed;
you've failed to act responsibly on debt.

We've waited patiently to get your check.
Contact us now about a payment plan.
You've failed to act responsibly on debt.
Let's make a deal—you pay us what you can.

Contact us now about a payment plan
before we move this matter into court.
Let's make a deal—you pay us what you can,
but pay us now, no more attempts to thwart

this debt. We'll move this matter into court
if that is what it takes to make you pay.
So pay us now, do not attempt to thwart
the payment process with further delays.

Is this what it takes to make you pay?
Your credit privileges won't be renewed.
All payments will be processed without delays.
We've yet to hear from you with payment due.

THE PAYOFF

Instant riches, lucky numbers, my father knew
those games—horse races, scratch-off cards—
his fever rose as jackpots grew.

Not one ticket, not merely two,
he bought as many as he could hoard.
Instant riches, lucky numbers, my father knew

a life of trying to accrue
the kind of luck he couldn't afford.
His fever rose as jackpots grew.

Every night he would review
a pile of tickets he'd discard.
Instant riches, lucky numbers, my father knew

the lure of easy revenue—
compulsion hit my father hard.
His fever rose as jackpots grew.

He spent his cash as bills came due
with losing tickets his reward.
Instant riches, lucky numbers, my father knew
his fever would rise as jackpots grew.

Signatures

My mother's handwriting was crabbed
and small, nothing like the elegant flourishes
my father used to sign his name,
his curlicues and fancy loops
far more feminine than Mother's scrawl.
He called it chicken scratch, as if it were
some defect of character to have such
handwriting, him the moral superior
for having learned proper cursive.
He had the kind of signature
you'd expect to see on money,
power in decorous grasp.
My mother had a child's writing,
letters collapsing in on themselves,
crawling off the page in scattered bits
of code. She wrote lefthanded,
penmanship made even more difficult
after she broke her writing arm
in a childhood fall from a tree.
Now all I do is write about them,
about losing them, no more notes
in either hand, no undisciplined script
from her, no haughty inscriptions
from him, no more evidence I came
from people who sometimes
wrote something down, words
that might be as simple
as a name, a number, a date of birth.

A Daughter's Villanelle

If you could read these words, I'm sure you'd damn
me straight to hell for everything I've said.
I write about your life because I can.

What right have I to criticize your plans,
wring poems from the life I think you led?
If you could read these words, I'm sure you'd damn

my college education, or the white man
I never even told you that I wed.
I write about your life because I can.

Should I have stayed at home, tried to withstand
your shifts in mood from joy to rage to greed?
If you could read these words, I'm sure you'd damn

the talent that I waste trying to scan
the junk of memory for what I need.
I write about your life because I can,

because I couldn't live as you'd demand.
But you can't read these words. My father's dead,
and cannot read the words I'm sure he'd damn.
All I can do is write, because I can.

ACKNOWLEDGMENTS

The author wishes to thank the following publications
in which these poems first appeared:

Kestrel: How Sweet the Sound," "The First Moment,"
  "Countrymen"
The Peralta Press: "A Daughter's Villanelle"
The Formalist: A Journal of Metrical Poetry:
  "First Birthday After Your Death: November
  1998," "In the Funeral Parlour," "Before the
  Burial"
Ellipsis: "Greeting Cards"
Atlanta Review: "My Father's Kites"
Limestone Circle: "Absence Without Leave"
Pleiades: A Journal of New Writing: "The Payoff"

 Born in London, England to parents of Caribbean heritage, ALLISON JOSEPH lives, writes and teaches in Carbondale, Illinois, where she directs the MFA Program in Creative Writing at Southern Illinois University Carbondale. She also serves as editor and poetry editor of *Crab Orchard Review*, a national journal of literary works, and director of the Young Writers Workshop, a coed residential creative writing summer workshop for high-school aged writers. She also serves as moderator of the Creative Writers Opportunities List, an online list-serve that distributes calls for submissions and literary contest information to writers free of charge.

She is the author of five previous books of poems: *What Keeps Us Here* (1992, winner of the Ampersand Press Women Poets Series Prize and the John C. Zacharis Prize from Ploughshares and Emerson College), *Soul Train* (1997, Carnegie Mellon University Press), *In Every Seam* (1997, University of Pittsburgh Press), *Imitation of Life* (2003, Carnegie Mellon UP), and *Worldly Pleasures* (2004, winner of the Word Press Poetry Prize). She is also the author of a chapbook, *Voice: Poems*, published in 2009 by Mayapple Press. She has received fellowships and awards from the Bread Loaf Writers Conference, the Sewanee Writers Conference and the Illinois Arts Council.

CPSIA information can be obtained at www.ICGtesting.com
Printed in the USA
LVOW01s0012181113

361574LV00001B/30/P